D0981721

# Raghead

# New Issues Poetry & Prose

| | |
|---|---|
| Editor | Nancy Eimers |
| Managing Editor | Kimberly Kolbe |
| Layout Editor | Danielle Isaiah |
| Assistant Editor | Samantha Deal |

New Issues Poetry & Prose
The College of Arts and Sciences
Western Michigan University
Kalamazoo, MI 49008

First Edition, 2019.

ISBN-13    978-1-936970-63-6 (paperbound)

Library of Congress Cataloging-in-Publication Data:
Hassan, Eman.
Raghead/Eman Hassan
Library of Congress Control Number          2018914469

| | |
|---|---|
| Art Director | Nicholas Kuder |
| Designer | Sarah Trumbull |
| Production Manager | Paul Sizer |
| | The Design Center, Frostic School of Art |
| | College of Fine Arts |
| | Western Michigan University |
| Printing | McNaughton & Gunn, Inc. |

# Raghead

Eman Hassan

New Issues Press

WESTERN MICHIGAN UNIVERSITY

*For my mother, Pauline, and my husband, Patrick, the bookend poets of my life*

# Contents

# Acknowledgements

*Blackbird*: "Invasion," "Suspended"

*The Blue Guitar*: "And Now, a Strange Concerto"

*The Boiler Room*: "For"

*Illuminations Journal*: "Subjectivism"

*KUDZU Review*: "To the Beach with My Nephew"

*Mizna*: "Forests Lean behind Us Now," "Slow Matricide," "Transport," "What We Made"

*Painted Bride Quarterly*: "I've Come Back for My Clothes"

*Stone Highway Review*: "To the Girl Who Flipped My Jeep"

*subTerrain*: "Raghead"

*Sukoon*: "A Different Kind of Hajj," "A Woman Not Paid in a Year," "Occlusions," "Singular Notes," "Swept Away"

## Rome Is Burning

I can't blame Nero for playing the fiddle

while watching his city fireball.

Sure, there was blood on his hands

turned powerless now

except for churning out tunes like a devil

dancing on a hot-oiled griddle.

It's not like everyone can hear the frantic

chirps of crickets.

We crank up our music at safe distances

from one another, take refuge

in front of a Blu-Ray Mesmer.

I mean, isn't this the stigmata of what we do?

All hail to purchase-power, to lifelines of credit.

All hail to the power of fire.

So play, Nero. Play that fiddle.

Let's break out some *Boom Chicka Pop* and watch

the world go—*poof!*

# I.

*Against the ruin of the world, there is only one defense: the creative act.*

—Kenneth Rexroth, *Disengagement*

# Hello, Patriarchy
*Kuwait, 2016*

An Arabesque road towards the sea will take you there.

Cross over Hwy 40 near Adan Hospital, straight into
the heart of an oil district.

Though interjected with roundabouts
this road seems infinite, seems circulatory, though

flanked by ginormous bins of crude black, fat as blood clots,
pumped fuller than capillaries.

A cardiovascularesqué history, everything is different
and so the same (*it's been so long since*)

though I can't remember the first time driving past
these white metal vats

along searing asphalt. To the distant right
there's a geometry of refinery pipes

piping their piston arms, pumping in systolic glugs…

…everything is different and yet the same.

No matter my commitment to ping-ponging between
continents. Here,

there's a constant hierarchy. Here, there are pathways
mapped by migrations,

by oil-bloomed neocolonialists (different), multi-national corporations, both foreign

and indigenous. By second- or third-generation biculturals, by the paperless (and so the same).

Above tarmac, the sun blares ubiquitous, indiscriminate in it's sizzle. Waves of heat

rise, consume, shimmer. No matter the blur of memory or crud of years. And so

· by the truck-fulls, sponsored migrant workers churn out fistfuls of revenue.

At the Avenues Mall stroll the emptied, saline sac-like post-war listless

herds of the voracious…

> …*Hello, patriarchy. Remember me?*

The road stretches as if it were going to run over—
*boil into me,*
                    into the blood-blue sea.

## War Starts at Home

There's alienation consequent to a bicultural marriage
without networks of a racial similar.

My father, *Raghead lover of that goat-herder.*
My mother, *that American whore.* War started at home.
Difference bred disrespect, spawned estrangement

from the other. Their offspring cleaved
when they fought, shrunk from their words—not those rosy petals
falling from their mouths when they broke

bread, but withered from thorny spillage of language
begetting violence.

When younger, *you look like your father, only
much prettier.* Or later, come college: *don't muddy my face, don't
shame us, like your mother.*

When the war left home I carried it
in my cleavage, across the planes of my face, into landscapes
of an otherness born of consequent alienation.

My visage grew strange in the mirror.
It birthed contempt. It looked for roses among violet bruises
each parent gifted to their *stupid lover.*

I was a whore. I was not a whore. And the world is at war.

# Invasion, 329 AM
*Kuwait, August 1990*

Under the glitter of morning's dusk, still drunk with my first lover's name.
Peering out behind blind slats, eleven stories up: I shouted Your Name.

Watched tanks tear in, blanketed by dregs of last night's dark stealth.
They tore through, those terrors from up North, and I forgot my name.

Forgot to breathe— my index finger spiraled digits on our rotary phone.
Left voicemails, incoherent messages, trying to recall everyone's name—

Loved ones casual friends I woke my father before morning's call to prayer.
An *athaan*, my uncouth mouth shaped heresy, damning Saddam's name.

My speech shaken, struck in aphasia-like shock— my words siphoned, even.
But until that day of my unbinding, I'll keep saying that first love's name.

For weeks blasts shook air. Panes shivered. Skylines were pummeled, razed.
August dust, white-heat sizzle. Kuwait City: bombed into a lack of name.

Weeks and weeks, deep under occupation, rifle butts split lips, caved in skulls.
Faces hushed, but those rifles, relentless. Corpses bloated, nameless.

Years later, bullets ricochet, whirr, pass through my mind, past emblazoned faces.
My father, shouting *Sshh-lower your eyes! Give those soldiers a fake name.*

My "I" silenced, though since my eyes speak Anger. Tidal rages grip my brain.
Lifetimes after, I still have forged IDs somewhere: my face, an Iraqi name.

On the dreaming side, heads reassemble: out of ditches, dust, from pulp, into form.
Those faces, me, we rise as one, chanting, "We Shall Never Forget" our names.

Once briefly named "nineteenth province", in lieu of our country's stolen one.
Know me, here: *bint al-Hakim*, always: my name spelled backwards is *name*.

# Guns & Lemon Trees
*Kuwait, September 1990*

We dug deep into the night,
tunneling beneath two lemon trees

inside the front yard,
piles of soil around us growing in the dark

like mounds on fresh plots
we dug furiously, bit back whimpers

if someone stubbed a toe,
splintered a finger, us girls, our father,

shoveled in the dark, digging
and digging to backdrop sounds

of creaking, pendulous bodies swinging,
ropes around their necks

under streetlamps, outside the front
wall: our neighbor's men, alit, swaying

in light nocturnal breezes,
tongues blue and long now they never told

on anyone, even when
their gun stash was discovered, in the back

of a *kengiyya*, the storage space
above the *diwanniya* bathroom. I remember

that windless day.
The whole street was forced to watch them

brought out, first
made to kneel then strung up, after

someone's suggestion.
Entire families' of men, the women spared

for something later.
The whole street was forced to watch,

watched them drop
from lampposts. I remember the snap

of necks, watching their light dim
beneath unlit bulbs: on pain of death no one

dared cut them down so they
swung, outside our front yard wall as we

dug deep, dug furiously,
listened to those women's grieving interrupted

with protests against
their own assault, their wails another sonic layer

dropped onto the night's turntable,
into its remix: creaking ropes, sudden rise

of desert wind, dull thuds of shovels,
muffled screams behind windows only two

houses down. We kept quiet,
kept digging, dug deep, dug furiously

until the tunnels were readied,
filled with oil-clothed packages, relocated

from our backyard sewer:
44s, hand grenades, Kalashnikovs purchased

on the sly, homemade Molotovs,
ammunition, nine millimeters, silencers, clips,

rifles from back in the day
when my father hunted with Sami Montoya

on the outskirts of Las Cruces.
We packed dirt back in with our hands, feet,

after each gun was in,
landscaping out the evidence, unpotted

and replanted floral designs
of ful'la, jasmine, and lavender. I remember

how enormous cockroaches
swarmed out of the sewer four days later;

our turn for a surprise visit,
the stench of shit in afternoon heat

as its metal lid was pried open.
I remember those crowbarred, sweat-slicked

uniformed men, how
the admiral gave the all-clear while admiring

my blossoming breasts,
the way his fingers lingered when patting

my younger sister's head,
his mustached leer at our fresh flowerbeds.

I remember my heart thudding
in my chest at our narrow margin of days,

the way I clenched my fists
to hide dirt still under my nails, the way

I struggled to unclench fists,
how I struggled to still my fists, I remember

the admiral's heavy lips whistling the all-clear,
not finding any guns, telling my father

*how lucky you are to have daughters with gardening skills*
*instead of sons, who might have gotten you killed.*

# March for Peace & a Demonstration
*D.C., Fall 1990*

> *War is an anachronism maintained through advanced technology and manipulated*
> *emotions, on behalf of corporate power, in the name of chauvinism.*
> —Adrienne Rich, *A Human Eye*

Kuwaiti women in black sweatshirts
stand at the peripheries, the words *Free Kuwait*

emblazoned across their chests
in green, red and white text. They clutch signs

bearing slogans:
*It's Not About Oil But People* or *We Want Peace Too*

some hold pictures of victims,
tortured bodies needing no textual elaboration.

One poster reveals two
juxtaposed figures: Adolf Hitler & Saddam Hussein

both in military dress, posing with children.
Beneath them, *DON'T LET HISTORY REPEAT*

*ITSELF.* Meanwhile,
the march surges towards 600 Pennsylvania,

centipedes past their sideline huddle,
small chronologies of their lives rocked by waves

protesting military bases, jostled by chants
against oil prices, their bodies silent, standing ground

amid the tidal demonstration,
in a tactical agreement on demeanor and dress:
by-products of war, whored out for the press.

## Suspended
*Above Southern Kuwait oil fields, 1991*

The pilot misunderstood our silence

swooped the helicopter low for a closer look

the desert burning like candlesticks

weeks and weeks of night on end

we washed cars with gasoline to remove soot,

covered naked women in deserted police stations

after Saddam's soldiers withdrew.

*Is there another lunatic who says war*

*makes for a better person?*

They left pelicans oil-slicked, killed coral,

took truckloads of our men in their wake.

I recall that pilot as though trembling

before a forgotten lover's ghost,

remember only hovering above

slanted columns of billowing smoke,

a birthday's endless night.

# 251<sup>st</sup> Evacuation Hospital
*KKMC, Saudi Arabia*

The ongoing joke: our lives were like M.A.S.H.
characters', only in deserts

instead of jungles. We drew parallels
between the hospitals,

amusing distinctions over late night M.R.E.
repasts: beef stew, reconstituted

mashed potatoes, stale slices of white bread, dodgy
peanut butter lumps,

semblances of cheddar, padding our meals
with Doritos, Slim Jims.

The familiar grub got us through nights,
our days spent scuffing boots

down plastic halls of makeshift wards, 90 miles
from the Kuwaiti border.

I felt like an imposter, cast as Sergeant Interpreter
in a surreal production,

greeting helicopters full of wounded POWs
just like the sitcom:

*where does it hurt what is your name?* Then came
an influx of civilians,

along with post-war, anti-Baathist rebels
alleging they were rallied

by air-dropped pamphlets: George Bush, Sr.
promising military support

if they rose against Saddam Hussein (aka
"So Damn Insane"),

a backup that never materialized, their pressing,
PTSD-impressed *why nots*

and *how comes* I had no witty comebacks for.

## Police Station
*Kuwait, March 1991*

You can tell the Iraqis took off in a hurry
but the energy left behind

left our skin in prickles: bullet casings
littered rooms like confetti,

overturned desks, bookshelves, riddled
with gunshot holes, broken chairs,

chains, rope; pliers, car batteries, wire,
odd array of objects

in empty jail cells, cement floors stained
and telltale.

Naked women were forced to serve tea here,
ankles cuffed

then uncuffed when called to service.
I remember

a hardbound notebook catching my eye,
flapping pages

thick with illustrations, meticulous text,
its contents straining

the boundaries of my imagination: crude
sketches of electrode crowns,

glimpses of headers: *How to Scoop Out Eyes,*
or *Let's Mutilate Genitalia.*

Then there were indexes—best methods
for prolonging pain…

…You insist, *tell me,* but I can't remember
specifics:

all that time spent standing in the heat,
my head bent over

its graphic interior, now just a cold finger
on memory.

## Forests Lean behind Us Now
*Winter, 1990*

In Massachusetts we watched the dark
lasered with showers of green
across the TV screen
in great aunt Marie's gazebo;
Kuwaiti skies all backlit
with neon smoke of artillery
thinking of family still there
under the assault,
of our father, the day his *ghutra*
gyrated out the window
as my sister hit the gas pedal,
leaning out of the car, video cam
strapped to his shoulder,
the drawing back shot of soldiers
taking aim, firing,
sear of bullets whizzing over blasts
of our father's profanities
over the screech of tires
stench of burnt rubber
and him, laughing maniacally
in the background of shaky footage
as the triangle of white cloth flew
off his head, smacked
a gunman, ghosting his face,
deflecting punctuated rounds
and my sister's hands are shaking now
as she strikes a match
during the retelling, takes deep drags
off her Marlboro Red,
cloud of white smoke
escaping her

almost a shroud of depleted uranium.

## the gulf war happened
(A response to Baudrillard's, *The Gulf War Did Not Take Place*)

B: "What we saw was a clean war."

A: By the second day, a yellow malaria fevered looters at the Gold Souk. A desire to inflict bodily harm infected the dirt. In shoddy collaboration on sanitation disposal and dealing with the dead, the ground turned into landscapes of filth. Human refuse, fleshy remains, laced paved and bare earth. At the borders, restroom floors
overflowed with rivers of sewage.

B: "An apocalypse of real time & triumph of the virtual over the real."

A: When an ostrich sticks its head in sand it believes it's invisible. Here, the desert littered with landmines virtually transformed into an anti-Easter ground zero. Shrapnel of real human bones like nightmares scattered across dunes. Yes, images work like text. War is a real disaster, yes. Yes, a victory too, of Capital Gains over Value of individuals. No triumph here, except if you were literally
virtually standing over there.

B: "The logic of simulation."

A: It's fallacy those under occupation had access to video games. Cars became arcade flight decks, their wheels stuck in slippery slopes near Saudi borders, leaving entire families dead. It's plausible that on TV screens this looked like a military-themed movie, simulated a Halloween horror party.

Are you with me so far?

B: The Gulf War as a "relentless and preprogrammed military machine."

**A:** All reference to April Gillespie virtually disappeared from the Internet. Fact: that former U.S. ambassador told Saddam Hussein, *if Iraq invaded Kuwait, the U.S. was not obliged to interfere.*

**B:** "In the future it will be possible to read these essays as science fiction."

**A:** Yes.

## *el-Insaan min el-Nisyaan* (To be human is to forget)

1.

*A good memory is not so good as a little ink.*

There's a reckoning to be had in proverbs, those hindsight gems, twinkles of potential

for different outcomes, before causal choices are made along each way, all the way back

to that first jolted slap and ensuing wail, to the first embrace of eyes with another's,

fresh as a new coat of blackboard paint, brimmed with recognition before learning to hate,

before learning by rote, and text is chalked upon the slate.

2.

Take the potential for a second opportunity. *Knock knock.* Take February, 1991,

post-Liberation Day: an image of Kuwait's Emir at the airport, falling to his knees

as he wept and kissed tarmac, joy and devastation roiling behind his famous twinkle.

I believe his grief, in first-hand discernment of oil-blazed skies, was real:

how can that kind of homecoming, for any man or baby
not be?

There's no place like it, as the saying goes. Or take Clausewitz:
*peace as perpetuation of war.*

3.

Anyone brushed by warfare has the potential to know
War as a profit-making venture,

or to know it as a leveling, similar to that now-dead king's,
an instance even-keeled

as after the trauma of being birthed; a clarity before
the forgetting, though never

a proverbial quote ever able to sugar-coat the annihilation
war causes.

Take two soldiers, holding guns against the other's temple,
each chalked up

as *enemy,* eyes locked, hands steady, gazes embroiled
in a final twinkle of truth:

there's never a thing sweet or honorable about it.

## What We Made
*Kuwait, 2000*

Tiny pellets in glass jars on the CFO's desk & the desk
of the warehouse manager, who once proudly asked

my green-eared newbieness if I knew how important
our job was, if I knew *What We Made*

supplied raw material for grocery bags, Tupperware, milk
containers, lighters, you name it—*Plastic is in*

*everything*, he'd say, & he was right. There I learned various
petrochemical densities: *poly*propylene, *poly*ethylene,

& other by-products emitted like ammonia &
the eminent dangers sometimes-released ammonia clouds

posed. We were committed to stay indoors until those vapors
passed, but who can say for sure where they passed on

to? An older British man there took great pleasure in
pinching the backs of my hands, teaching me

about elastin: how the body's fibroblasts produce less & less
as we age. How he enjoyed my 20-something's horror

at the prospect of losing collagen. I'm not proud of who I was
then, nor proud of my former manager,

who laughed when I could no longer live with myself and quit:
she thought me a loser— & she was right,

except aren't we all losers in these long-term, climatic stakes?
Sometimes I think of those former co-workers, wonder

if, when settling before a lunch of grilled fish, they ever thought
(in addition to the cost of price per barrel),

of what the long-term costs of *What We Made* were: if they had seen
pictures of seagulls' desiccated gullets, splayed open,

cavities filled with tensile stuff, if they connected the dots between
plastic pellets in the bellies of fish warming their own stomachs:

*fruits de mer* of our own making.

## Slow Matricide
*Arizona, 2010*

My mother keeps pouring gasoline on her head,
keeps dousing her newly shaven

scalp with the stuff, wraps rags around
her nicked baldness

to keep the fumes in, tries to kill what she believes
are subcutaneous

lice infesting her follicles. No doubt she believes
they are real, when she blows

out matches, presses charred sticks to the razed
surfaces of her skull,

performs her own ritual of controlled burning,
after running a Bic razor

across her crown, sweeps crisp bits of scab
onto the coffee table. How many times,

how many times we've cajoled her to get help, stop
this ongoing fracking of her scalp.

But mother ignores us, pooh-poohs the doctor's
diagnoses, holds up

a magnifying glass, scrutinizes the detritus before her,
jowls set, beneath a fiery

beet-red, pomegranate head, insists she sees corpses
in her own Rorschach-evident test.

Driving from Flagstaff, I'm detoured by devouring
forest fires, and think *what if we are all wrong:*

what if our mother is the only one who got it right,
despite her suicidal, death drive fight?

Acrid smoke fills the air and all I can see are orange
flames, the crash of timber resonating

omens.

## To the Beach with My Nephew
*Highway 30, 2004*

It's in the way we hold a sandwich
in each hand: we relished the drive, my sister recalling how light blue
were the skies of our youth, turning backs on the soot-heavy black

                        now spewing from the Ahmadi Oil Refinery we pass by:
        uncapped flares smoking like dirty dinars, lighting the desert on fire

for more. The refinery resembles New York City at night to those who know

and dream of being somewhere else, maybe over there
though we savor the cheap falafel wraps over here.

Once we reach the shore, I tell Little Ant how clean the deep used to be.

Now barnacles form
     on Styrofoam,
                    wind hurls the white-tipped whorls forward
like a heartbeat,
like a refinery
that never sleeps.

I want to say *Enough, oh Sea,* like that b&w Kuwaiti movie, but waves keep coming.

Two hermit crabs are locked in battle:
it's in the way their claws grip together.

My nephew meant well, jumped to interfere,
save the smaller from becoming
the larger one's meal

                  but the waves keep coming and we are in Manhattan
                  looking out a window over the Hudson.

# Occlusions

i. *What we leave out.*

I know something of that clank,
nickels, pennies in my mouth
rusting at the back of my throat—
makes me think of rosebushes
along my backyard wall
my urge to clip their unruly babel of leaves
down to an original stump
and I am lost
in shrubberies of my own language,
held back by arbitrary branches.
At night I brush twigs from my bushy hair,
pull thorns from under my tongue.
Makes me think of my grandmother,
when turning seven, seeing speech
as perception, announced
to her immigrant mother, *no more Polish*
*will be spoken at home again: only American.*
She taught me how to swear
in her maternal tongue, often spoke
of how Great Nana Julia
would scream
long strings of words
at her husband, monosyllabic, compound phrases
in a language she didn't remember,
just cuss words
arbitrarily passed down.
My mother shares this one night, nodding off,
smiling at the memory of her grandfather Stanislaus,

mumbling as he stands up in dramatic pause,
looks down at his screechy wife, flips his hearing aid off.

ii. *Loose change.*

Some people in the old Kuwaiti market
mistake me for American,
which I am, but also one of them,
unlike my British brother in-law,
who teaches Arabs to speak English
at thirty-five dollars an hour,
his price half the cost
the institute he worked at
charged for his cockney.
Even he can hear my words
as different, almost off-key,
softer on the gutturals
and heavier intonations. Yes,
I tell him, yes, I am lost between
the diphthongs of one language
and another, among three-pronged
Arabic's roiling lyric, and Anglophone
Latin, who's various roots twist
and branch plural versions
British or American English, yes,
I am lost in my own lack
of a single linguistic socialization.

Who are we, peering out from a construct of sentences,
giving them jingle and form? Who can put a price to our coins?

iii. *What we take for granted.*

At T-Mobile I single Elton out,
his lilt: Elton is Chaldean,
from the land of Babel and Sumer.
He's never been, but wants to be
an interpreter in Iraq: the money,
he heard, was good. When his manager
steps back into the room Elton stops
the conversation, says loudly
he was born in Michigan,
explains my messaging service
will let me text Kuwait
at forty-five cents a pop.
Elton pronounces *Kuwait*
like the noun is made of money:
reminds me how we take for granted
the wealth of a multiple language.
Elton reminds me of my father
who never took the Lord's name in vain
but praised it, often switching
compound words in English, saying
*towel paper* or *stew Irish.*
He took for granted I'd be
proficient in Arabic, dismayed
at my syntactic variations.
I took for granted our final conversation
mostly out of shock, while we watched
the broadcast of the kidnapped US contractor
on TV, too stumped to speak.

*What we leave out or take for granted. What we take in vain.*
The way they held a knife under Nick's throat, ululating His Name.

# Raghead
*Kuwait, 1988*

It was more than penis envy, more than ancestral calling
of desert warriors, who understood

the power those filmy layers had to survive the sun's
overwhelming

but oh man, the tactile allure of phyllo fabric between fingers
still thrills me.

Castration complex, straight-up sexual attraction—
no matter, but I used to don

my father's headgear, preen in his bedroom mirror
(*mmm, how handsome!*),

my pulse pounding in Bedouin drumbeat fashion,
afraid to wrinkle its starched goodness

or be found in its gauzy tabernacle, admiring
how white material

flanked my profile like holy sideburns, stiff wings
halo-like, delicate when left

hanging. I was outrageous in my faux drag,
feeling like a deck hand

struggling to master the art of a sail-flip
over a shoulder.

Just a curious teenager, bored over summer break, desirous
of my first dishdasha experience,

lip-synching Boy George: *karma karma karma chameleon!*
Or pretending I was a nun

in habit, wagging a finger at my reflection in bouts
of mid-summer night's imagining—

*get thee to a nunnery!*

No matter my precaution, my father finally caught a show
of my shenanigans, zeal of his pleasure

at my make-believe surreal as he taught me to fold
the cloth, tease its front

into a dent, under an anchoring rope of *gahfiyya.*
He dressed me up in a dishdasha

and we went for a ride. He let me drive the whole stretch
of Gulf Road, agreeing my name

for the night was Ibrahim el-Majnoon…

…and crazy we were, with my eyeliner'd uni-brow,
penciled moustache,

and him, still loud and lively, pretending I was the son
he didn't have.


Oh *ghutra:* to me, you are everything but a rag.

## Dishdasha Experience
*Kuwait, 2002*

DJ swore he would never be caught dead
in native garb.

Boy, was he adamant. *I'm no damn raghead!*
he'd yell, eyes half-open,

when I'd observe, *how striking the contrast,*
his goatee's chocolate

next to alabaster skin. I am beige as a biscuit,
but DJ was pale

as his tea-dumper lineage. DJ turned on
the music: we wore sameness,

both chicken nuggets–slang for half-breeds:
brown outside, white in.

Both liminal, rebellious, donning masks
that cleaved like Janus,

more—much more, than either side's sum
of our otherness,

I made roses from ragweed, but to DJ
the effort was tedious.

He preferred to peer at the world
under a Red Sox cap,

holding his pain closer than an enemy,
cocooned in illusory

musical tracks. Years later, they found DJ
dumped in a dim-lit parking lot,

lips swollen blue, face ashen, chest covered
in purple-fisted attempts

at resuscitation, stripped of the previous
night's denim;

as if someone had hurriedly dressed him
in that ill-fated dishdasha.

## Borders & Boundaries

Meanwhile, beneath a man-made wall
snakes slither,

scorpions scurry across Sonoran Desert floors.
Half-way across the world,

a mother and daughter hold hands in secret
through a chink

in a different partition. Every morning
they do this. Meanwhile,

above The Great Wall of China, sky dwellers
unencumbered by delineations

of men; don't recognize no-fly zones,
while rolls of barbed wire

hook along tops of prison camp fences,
enclosing men:

a panopticon of incarceration
in biopolitical existence

their labor outsourced to corporations
for cents on the dollar.

---

Once, the walls of Kout City's boundaries
kept warring invaders

outside its fortress, kept their territorial claim
and occupants safe,

long before demarcations on maps entered
their awareness.

Now it's geckos and jerboas who are free,
just as termites,

colonies of ants in subterranean cities
who are free, living within

their citadel's clandestine enclosures:
living off productions

of their specious labor, culled from topsoil
firmaments…

…To know the purpose of mountain ranges
is no small thing. To know

the legacy of capitalism, the flagged,
carved-up, post-colonial,

squabbled-over parcels, drawn on parchment
is no small thing.

Ø Ø Ø Ø Ø

Google maps have given us the illusion
of a rotund pie, sliced

indefinitely. Meanwhile, animal species
not yet farmed by us roam

under, march through, across, and over
state lines, through

road blocks, check points, country borders,
not acknowledging

our grandiose propriety. In the end, all
control over spatial territory

devolves into a cartography of pine box,
a hole in the ground,

an oven, a giving up of boundaries,
our bodies; a slip beyond

the last line, all physical concept of space
minds can't imagine.

****

Does the world belong to us, or do we
belong to the world?

Over the span of my life I've known
stateless people,

met a man who owned three passports.
I have seen boats

full of refugees tear-gassed on TV, turned back
to sea. I've known

the tethers of corporate cubicles. Still,
I dare dream,

believe in the collective potential to remember
the simplicity of a life still

bound with nature, without framed
artifices of borders.

# II.

*(I know you: you're the one who's bent so low.*
*You hold me—I'm the riddled one—in bondage.*

*What work could burn as witness for us two?*
*You're my reality. I'm your mirage.)*

—Paul Celan, *La Contrascarpe*

# Distillation Poem
*Kuwait, Active-Present*

Everything is different and yet the same.

The same moon arcs across skies less
and less blue, while vanity mirrors

still reflect an ever-constant *me me me*, still
deflect backgrounds of sponsored Asians in bondage.

Fingers of moonlight grow long across dressing tables,
wrap eyes in gossamer bandages...

... if you're looking for a sonnet, this isn't it.

Come, take your pill and remember
those petrified lessons of war's carnage, come

smell the putrid outpouring of sewage, still let
into the sea, in the dim-lit dead of night,

raw as the dead who now see
standing behind each shoulder like worried angels

longing for fingers to touch, to unfasten the knots
at the backs of our skulls...

## Swept Away
*Kuwait, 2016*

These are the colors of a country
rippling below its glorious flag,
not red, not green, not black or white
but yellow, bright yellow, only
bright yellow jumpsuits sweeping
through the streets, rippling

in the car-stirred wind, jumpsuits, not men,
hard to tell them apart, their Asian faces,
indistinct as the accumulated
refuse they sweep into overfed refuse

bags: hard to tell them apart
bright yellow garbage bags
bright yellow jumpsuits
both branded with
interchangeable company logos:
*Clean-Co*             *Tanzif-Co*

branded by equally interchangeable bloated bellies:
over-stuffed garbage sacks
hunger-puffed jumpsuits
blurred in the mechanical breeze of passing cars:
*Mercedes*             *Jaguars*

passengers zoom by, unmoved, refuse
to notice the exchangeable bags
acknowledged only through the daily gift
of trash: empty candy wrappers
cigarette butts or soda cans: daily bread
collected by an invisible hungry man.

So that the duress of an empty yellow sleeve
does not disturb, you roll up
your windows at the traffic light,
look right through the bodiless dress, as you
must, fluttering beneath palm trees, sweeping
out the debris of the day, eating dust.

These are the colors of a country
rippling below its glorious flag.
A collective dirty secret.
A state. Colors of Kuwait.

## And Now, a Strange Concerto

Harp, what sounds you make
through your heavy bow-bent back, strung out
to reconcile wire and wood.

You could have been a trumpet
bellowing your life's music, instead a winged clavicle
of conflicting tunes.

As if you were a guitar,
warped along the frets of your strained wood neck,
spoiling every bar. And if you

think you are immune,
weird harp, know that you too are a strange instrument,
no stranger than a cactus,

not yet able to sing,
raising its prickly arms to desert skies, whispering
*por favor, I am thirsty.*

# Coins & People

Spinning coins fall either way and so do people.


Some people will dance for coins
thrown at them. Then there are people

who like to throw coins
down & make others dance. Some people

will dance hot & heavy for coins
until the dance grows venomous, grows

brutal, until heads crack, tails
break. Some knowingly watch, refuse to join in;

others move to a different rhythm,
preferring passionate tangles of tangos,

arms folding into the other's tempo,
waltz together as magnets. There are those

who don't get it & linger
on corners, weep for coins from strangers

& will not dance, those who exit
the dance with weights of coins on their eyes.

Some people's eyes never see coins
while others have so many coins they can't see

people. Some only know people
for their coins & though coins often flip

most people's heads & change choreographs
into staggers, we somehow forget how this story ends…


… it's always the same story between coins & people.

# Transport

Traffic on the road is terrible, but here this is normal.

This can be anywhere in the Middle East, the heat a stampede through

the solar plexus.

I see those men as I get in a cab, sink into cool air...

how those men stare—and I let them. I can see—

not *through*, but *at*: I look on *to*.


And it startles their Asian faces enough
to momentarily forget how they sit, squashed, bent over
in small seats, shackled by space, shoulders numb against
sides of the metal truck...

you know, the kind used to move livestock.


Trafficking on the road is terrible, but here this is normal.

This can be ... anywhere in the Middle East.

*Eyes peek out of parallel slats*
                                    *as if peering from an oven.*

# Homo Sacer
*Kuwait, 2002*

> *n.* A sacrificial body that is outside the juridical protection of
> the law, and as a result is subject to extreme violence.
> —*Antonio Agamben,* Homo Sacer

After her highway manslaughter
Alia comes to work late
wearing a white hijab
she wore a white dress too
as she zigzags between offices,
hands out chocolates.
Alia gave the good kind
from *Leonidas,* costly truffles,
caramels, to anyone who'd listen
to her *poor-me* tales. She did this
the way someone gave candy
for an engagement, promotion,
or birth of a baby,
wearing a baby-like smile
as she passed around sacraments,
imported delicacies, swathed foils
in an array of autumn colors.

Alia explained how his death
was *halal:* kosher. He wasn't Muslim,
*not even from one of the Three Religions.*
She simpered about inconveniences:
filing a police report, a banged-up
Lexus jeep garaged for three days.
I could tell what Alia means to say
is the man she killed was no one really,
just a sponsored Bengali street cleaner

in a polyester uniform, an imported body
to clean up our mess and *what was he thinking,*
*crossing the highway on foot like that?*

Rust-orange and coppery reds
swapped from her hand to my desk
wink in shrouded conspiracy: wrappings
worthy of imported Dutch delicacies.

# Found & Forgotten

*From the U.N.'s* Universal Declaration of Human Rights

"Whereas recognition
of the inherent dignity of
the equal & inalienable rights
of all members of
the human family


is the foundation of freedom, justice, and peace in the world,


whereas disregard
and contempt for human rights
have resulted in barbarous acts
which have outraged
the conscience of mankind."

# A Woman Not Paid in a Year
*For Banu Begum, 2008*

Shuffles through the halls of Adan Hospital
Is armed with a mop
Does her rounds in over-sized janitorial hand-me-downs
Reveals bulging eyes that burn with hunger
Scans food trays for leftovers
Grabs anything salvageable
Guzzles warm Pepsi from half-empty cans in waiting rooms
Wonders if anyone hears her stomach churning
Asks to be paid, is told next week, Inshallah
Pushes around a bucket of dirty water
Grinds her mop & imagines spaghetti carbonara
Believed lies the recruiter in Bangladesh told
Daydreams of mango trees back home, of gorging on sweet flesh
Wants to know why people in Kuwait are okay with this
Has no illusion anyone sees her
Will have toothpick arms
Works 14-hour shifts
Can't believe I can
See her
Wonders can she take the dregs of my shampoo bottle—
Hasn't had any in a year
Wears a hijab because *Clean Co.* makes her
Whispers of Bangladeshi deportations, kicked out for going on strike
Shares a cot with two other women
Sleeps in shifts
Is wound taut as a mouse trap
Is trip wire
Is waiting to be tripped
Still loves a man she knew at sixteen
Wears hard lines around a gaunt jaw at twenty-six
Dreams of being looked deep in the eyes
Wants me to take her to America
Translates her name as *Great Lady*

Is a bone shard spiked under my sternum.

# Madam (Madhavati)

*Baqer said the government would ensure workers were paid their regular salaries. And if any injustice happened to them, then they should go to the relevant authorities.*
—Kuwait Times, *August 6, 2008*


1- Madam
sips her tea
over the morning
newspaper, skims over
sections on traffic violations
(having nothing to do with her),
the screaming front-page headlines:
*Revolution of the Hungry Begins*
*Bangladeshi Workers on Strike*
*Thirteen Months: Still No*
*Salaries Paid.*

2- Madhavati
cries into her tea
every morning, ever since
her back was broken
when Madam pushed her
out a second-floor window
for breaking a crystal glass.
Four months still in Adan Hospital
forty monthly dinars
never paid.

1- Madam
thinks of her new lawn
inside the outer gate: imported

fresh grass from New Zealand
a green carpet to roll over the local
top-soil of her yard, her headscarf
fallen to her shoulders, wonders
whether the fresh grass will take
                    this time.

    2- Madhavati,
sweet as her namesake garden vine,
lies in her hospital bed, thinking
of the children she left behind
for a better life, food, money.
She thinks of *Mary*—her new
'easy to pronounce' name, given by Her
        when she first arrived.

    Ø- Mary,
played her unrecognized part perfectly
in her matching parlor uniform, Mary,
a shorter name to match
the coffin-wide room
where she once slept
in her sponsor's dream home.
The illusion shatters like a
            window pane.

    1- Madam's
house *boy*, an eternal *boy*
unsexed, waters the newly
imported lawn. He can see how

bare hair covers her shoulders
as she calls to her newer maid
for more tea: "Mary!"

1- Madam
thinks, "he won't dare look."
(*what is covered*)
Being a man, he looks.
(*is uncovered*)

"What matter, then, if the boy can see?
No shame except in front of men."

***

What is covered
is uncovered.

*Oh, tell it, tell it,*
says the Paraclete,

*peel back
the false self's lies…*

Like motes of dust

we rise.

# Absence
*Kuwait, 2006*

Body bent,
pinned face-down
across the screen
in Faisal's palm:
if you look closely
her form discloses
exactly what she
means to say, though
hard to tell what is
actually said,
her contorted pose over
the red kitchen freezer
at odds with the camera's
angle.
      Perhaps simply,
*I just want to go home*
is what's being said
despite the coy
female inflections
projected
from the phone:
a dubbed-over mouth
emits out-of-sync shapes
grating against the sound
of playful laughter,
against the statement,
*Sir, madam is going to come*
meaning, in this case, a
wife, mother, or sister
on their way home.
      Hers is no
ecstatic posture
of homemade porn.

In this video clip,
audio contradicts
the visual, blurring
what is between
two streams of senses.
The only utterances
we hear
is a voice-over impostor,
super-imposed
on an otherwise silent
background. Surely,
there were other sounds
taking place? Noises
that make one notice
the expressions on her face?
          Perhaps muted
sniggers of the one filming,
a slap or grunt from
the lead man, an electric
hum from the fridge
singing in tune
to her body language:
the pan that got knocked
over; surely any sound
other than *Sir, madam*
*is going to come,*
anything other
than the flirtatious
female laughter, caught
in perpetual loop
from the palm
of Faisal's hand:
a continuous rape
in the absence
of real sound
conditioned eyes
fail to hear.

## Portrait: Family with Knives
*Indeterminate Kuwaiti beach, 2014*

It took two to hold the turtle down,
a third to saw
and hack, taking turns
cheering each other
on a moonlit shore.
In the background
a woman claps, a child yells
claims to the severed
head.
I remember how as a kid
clutching bits of soggy bread,
we'd use bare hands
to catch minnows,
lure them into
our fisted tunnels
under the water's
surface, thumbs up,
poised to clamp,
take hold and revel
in brief delight
of their scaly wriggles.
In the end
we'd release them,
return each one whole.
The EPA offered
a 10K reward
to whoever named
those bandit relatives
in the YouTube clip,
their brutal slaughter
of an animal on
the Endangered
Species list,
unaware as one
taking pleasure

in a nocturnal stroll
along the beach
might be,

reveling in the prickle of sand between their toes.

# Gender Segregation Law
*After The American University of Kuwait, 2004*

*The thought of a zigzag but moving straight in a circle.*

This image bounces through my mind,
knocks on the storage closet of memory,
flimsy door—

where I am still the crash dummy
in a classroom chair, testing how low
we can build mobile partitions, stretch

the laws of physics:

boys to one side,
girls on the other—

two inches less and if we strained our heads
our eyes could pretend
the paneling wasn't there.

Against the natural grain, yes:
we subjected the wood to interpretation
bent the planks of reason,

mounted them on wheels
without warping the frame.
The day turns around and folds

back into itself; I still feel the dent marks
across the broom closet
carpet of my own brain.

It was branches and growth rings we needed,
not sawdust-covered mottos
of *Learn. Think. Become.*

Not this backward sunlight rolling over modern
buildings of glass and steel,
becoming undone.

## The Blossoming
*For Malalai Joya: NYC, 2007*

She closes her eyes and sees
the beloved flowers of her garden
she will never look on again—
the lilacs, jasmine, and iris
—suddenly revealed
after enduring winter.

She sees women, some of them
walking miles to come and touch her,
as if her bravery might lend their mettle
its glint, steel their cores; a promise
they can feel in a place where affection's petals
are more scarce than poppies for opiates.

When she closes her eyes, she recalls
rosebud girls threatening to burn their faces,
begging her to end the cleaving to old men—
and mothers, with wringing hands, afraid for them;
she takes it in, absorbs their grief into her garden-depth
Zen, and while promising, smiles.

When she closes her eyes, she sees the men
lining the halls of parliament, shouting
*Rape her! Kill her!* Warlords bent on having her
head, their glares edgy as swords swooping
through her garden the night she fled,
as if, in shedding the *burga*, she unveils

them; lays bare the blade of their lens,
unlocks the violent selves that, in seeing
the self reflected for the first time,

try to smash her instead.
All those years, while controlling the very breath,
the cloth did not penetrate her mind.

She does not cower, stands tall on the stalk
of her intent, under the heat of their blood-lust gaze
stemming from a flowering
they deeply deny, as if her free face
were a vagina she flaunts, asking for it,
every time she closes her eyes.

# To the Girl Who Flipped My Jeep
*Kuwait, 2008*

It's not fireflies, I tell you.
Not blinking lights on graveled roads
filled with thorny briars

no valley of dinosaur eggs
your jeweled pirate's chest
pricks my ribs

secretly tucked
neuropathic highway signals
fray vertebra into discs.

Listen, the body
is barbed wire and dandelion,
synapse and tendon

driftwood composite
your delicate
architecture

my red handkerchief of bones.

# Without an Iota
*Nebraska, 2015*

The last time I saw that squirrel, he'd been sitting
beside the wrecked home I watched him build
with scraps autumn afforded,

carefully nestling leaves, twigs, in a fork of bark
outside my living room window. The last time I saw him
before then, he'd carefully wrapped

his house in strips of a plastic grocery bag caught
in that tree. I'd watch that squirrel while hiding—not so he
wouldn't see me, but because

that kind of watching seemed invasive. But I looked
anyway, cheering his Chewbacca face on, discretely drawing
the blinds so he'd continue thinking his high home

was inviolate: it was in my power to afford him
this small peace of mind. The last time I saw him months later
(and this time really the last), he was stretched out

on a branch beside his trashed home, without
an iota of self-pity, the debris of his labor not withstanding
the brutal charnel of a Midwest winter. There he was,

proud body catching rare winter sun, unruffled
in the knowledge that neither he nor the rubble of his sanctuary
would last the season. That squirrel made me grateful

for my slapped-together apartment, on the edge of Lincoln,
Nebraska's ghetto, glad for the rickety architecture
of my clumsy body somehow still holding together.

I've not seen that squirrel come out of his leafy mess
since then, but I've kept a lookout anyway,
left offerings of almonds beneath our tree, just in case.

# Dear Whinny and Shudder
*Puerto Penasco, Mexico, 2014*

Red brocade obscures my view
but on the shore I still catch the glint
in a pervert's eyes,
find unreserved love in a father's.

There's a man on a horse who wants me
to admire his muscles, his mare
whinnying with each kick given to her;
Mr. Muscles isn't the only one

who knows the trick
of using sound as a hook.
Hawk Eyes try to catch my eye
murmur, *Something free for you?*
As his jewelry jingles.

What catches my look is a simple rock,
its glisten compelling me to pick it up.
*There really is something free for me,* I marvel,
other than what those men hock.

Even birds know this sonic trick, know
to keep quiet around humans
when they must. *Be careful*

*of us, dears,* I boomerang this thought.
Later, I remember the way the vendor
stroked the V of his crotch,
something I hadn't let myself really see:

*something free for you* takes on a new
innuendo. I want to tell the father to look out
for the man watching his daughters
turn cartwheels,

craning for a glimpse of fantasy
between young thighs. *Dear rock.*
I want to tell Mr. Muscles

to give up, slap the leering vendors.
*Dear whinny and shudder.* Even pigeons at the pool's
edge are wary of boys who turn mean at a drop.
*Dear birds. Dear red brocade. Dear ears. Dear eyes.*

Dear pedophile: you too were once a boy.

# III.

*Human energy, which is consciousness, the capacity to produce change in existing conditions.*

—Muriel Rukeyser, *The Life of Poetry*

# Rome Is Still Burning

i.

Fiddlesticks to testimony:

we have only apocryphal narratives,
hearsay, documented

as facts, accounting for Nero's
whereabouts

on that infamous night. Some wrote
he was out of town. Others say

he played the fiddle while watching
the city burn.

Or those historians, valuing their heads,
depict him

pulling bodies from rubble instead of
ordering the striken match.

Here's what we know for sure: Truth
remains Artifact buried

under an oasis of the past.

These are the known facts:
Rome blazed,

death tolls most likely inaccurate.
We know lives

were lost, the particulars of which
in the machinations

of myth-making, are insignificant
granules of sand.

There's consensus that Nero murdered
his mother, though

she leveraged his rise to power.
We are told

she minted gold coins with Nero's image
after Claudius adopted him.

Later, coins with both their faces
on either side.

ii.

Fact: Power rises like wildfire.

Fact: Roman stone smoldered
        for days.

iii.

I prefer to think Nero played the fiddle
in the way fiddlers

at wakes make music, was also
a heroic artist,

not just a monstrous product of power
the trajectory of power

is known to catapult people into.

In this retelling there's an itch, deep
in the nostril

of Nero's dream, picking him out of
a webbed slumber,

where resinous scents of elderberry
and dandelion wine

are overpowered by char, singed hair,
smell of burnt flesh

and fabric, cloying the air of his
chambers,

yanking him awake to mend
his human disconnect,

lifting lunatic illusions of superiority
power brings

that clung like smoke. Those odors
jolt him

back into the smallness of when he
was a boy,

still possessed of that fierce sweetness,
joy in being

that inspires hands and hearts of artists.

He takes to the roof, where the city night
is overcome

with clamors of many-tongued flames
roaring from windows,

consuming buildings, people, their labor,
hot licks

growing closer.

iv.

In this story Nero is both hero and villain.

In my story Nero is alone.

He is having a moment of clarity.
He is experiencing momentary madness,

sees his predicament as at once beautiful
and absurd,

feeling powerless as one laid bare
before the possibility

of death might feel, when witnessing
travesty greater

than one's singular experience, lonely
without another beside him

to share in the spectatorship, perpetuate
the façade of emperor.

So he acts like any person stunned
out of their fixed narrative

might act, he picks up his fiddle, whittles
an homage to the flames.

*We retell this story over and over,*
*its winding repetition a spiraled staircase*

*echoing with footsteps.*

# Human Energy

*...the earth, the space between earth and sky. This space (the Osage)*
*called hó-e-ga, or snare of life...*
        —Garrick Bailey, *Osage & the Invisible World*

It's like a beam of light
caught in folds
of red velvet curtains,

a Vaquitas porpoise
tangled in
a fisherman's net

the beginning flutters
of song, stifled
behind pursed lips,

breaking into
the world, without zeal,
empty echo.

What can be done for a leaf
caught in an eddy?
Some call it

a dream, ready
to unravel upon
waking, liken it

to a Cubist painting,
how perspective
navigates the lines:

fragments going nowhere.

# Human Trajectory
*After Jan Fabre's* Lancelot, Knight of Despair

I'm in a white room in front of a screen,
watching Lancelot, caged in a dungeon
battling his reflection, cell of his mind
a tight fit
   but Lancelot, boxed in,
still manages a good fight against
his armored glint, drawing on his mettle
pits his sword against an enemy, as if,
among the punting clanks of metal
      on metal,
  he spars to the death, all hell-bent
in the dark, within a homegrown cage
of fear, the mind's invader, encircling
ribs, pierces his breath, as Lancelot rages
until spent, looped on repeat:

I'm in a white chamber before a screen.

# Subjectivism

The windshield smacks a sparrow. It falls stunned,
to the middle of the asphalt. Two-directional traffic
does not stop, but the bird revives and flies off.

There's a lesson here, I promise myself, and forget.

The cabbie tells me her name over and over—
all that sticks is she was a director at an Athens TV Station
six months ago.

At the Agora, drops of sweat trickle down
a bridge of nose. The tour guide regales us:
from an ancient Greek market a past filters

into present memory.

In the future my dollars are poor.
The moon's a little further there's no more Euro
and I'm already old
my speech outdated
patterned with *now*

encapsulating a time that was, is
to the impending old news.

Somewhere in India a driver passes a dead donkey.
Rolls down a Bentley window, throws a fistful of rupees
to children running behind his car. Waterfalls

plummet. Dams hold back, amass, limit.

Then there are days when water is butter
you can't tell the horizon from waves

the blur delicious
in contrast to billboard myths.

How to articulate this ache
full as clouds dark with water are...

...Perhaps all this a concept, sprung
from Hera's naughty head,

trickling down.

## To All People Ø

To the scientists: can we ever heal
this plasticized water?

To my mother: I already mourn
your not-yet death.

To mother earth: I say, my light
was once as big

as you are big, not a shriveled plum
skulking behind

its breast plate,
pumping out this spotty aura

deplete as the ozone.
To E.T.: yes please, *phone home*

—take me along, *sil vous plait?*
The empire is striking

hard, my words fallen angels
without halos,

my lightsaber now
just a glow stick, stuck in the back

corner of a drawer, left over
from the 90s.

To my generation X:
Did you forget what the X

even stood for? We were the ones
who invented the rave

and raved, gave big corps the finger,
danced ecstatically

under full moons:
we raged until the sun climbed over

a lip of earth. Those were right days,
we were grateful

for the radiant blessings of music
behind our force field

of youth. To all people:
don't you remember

the pre-spinning of words, like
*natural* and *free-range,*

when our biggest concern was lard
in Oreos, in a pre-Splenda,

pre-saturated, non-GMO era?
Better I hurry back

into my mother.
Better my mother hurry back into

her earth-womb, than stand witness
to all this, and all this.

## The World Is Screaming Now

Once    in Paris        alone
in love                 with Paris
I came across           a bridge
below                   Montmartre
crossing            over the Seine
its watermarked         cement
lit with graffiti       blaring
*The world is screaming*    *Now*
neon words      loom through
my memory               openings
my *Nows*               pinpoints

of sunlight    over        water.

## Kneading My Father's Rice Belly

It's been years since we've gathered around the foot
of your bed like this,

or spoke: one holds your hand, another massages your feet
swollen with too much rest.

Toffy reads some favorite prayers you'd read out loud
when we were children,

jumping like monkeys, kneading your rice belly
for our make-believe bread.

I sit to your left, as I once did at our table, feather-stroke
your forehead:

my fingertips are radars, heat sensors seeking to locate
that aneurism

spidering itself below thick bone. Deep down in your
lobes somewhere

you are still here, leaning into our voices, remembering,
and we are still

your monkeys, our untethered hands reaching, reaching...

# Gracelessly

Suddenly—
breath of spring barely exhaled—
pink lush petals of the *fresh ornament* turned pale yellow—

where did the time go?
Now how many poets have written on the *darling buds of May,* on *Violet
past its prime,* on

the flickering
blush of bloom, caught from an eye's corner instead of directly
apprehended, to say, e*verything that grows holds in perfection but*

*a little moment.*
Rather than pining for a dimple, green eyes or bigger breasts, you notice
furrows of *deep trenches in the beauty's field*

of your forehead,
those kilos you need to shed off your thighs because then you finally
will be beautiful. We take notice only in the leaving,

in the fleeting
departure of things, holding up hands to winter's light *of ragged defacement,*
taking note of growth rings around our knuckles.

# Speech Regrets

1.

Mostly I regret what I don't say,
ideas I itch to utter
swallowed instead

while my tongue, thickening,
swells with unsaids.
My windpipe's left coated

with bitters of regrets
aborted *I love yous,*
restrained expressions

—insights too,
 expostulations imploding
with each shortchanged moment

that uncrosses its legs
then tucks heels back
across my silent withholdings.

Oh, the exclamations
I've left stillborn. I rue them
more than articulations

I've let loose
but shouldn't, those thousand
bursts of batwings

spewing from the cave
of my ammonia'd mouth,
beating at air.

I repent my held back
words so much more
than these billows.

2.

I also have regrets
for the infidelities of my lips,
the spilled spelt,

cut glass of my vocals
spilt like indigestible
burnt bitters.

Disruption
within a silence
can't be unbroken,

just as an ear
can't un-hear, we can never
unsay, once the saying's

been said.
I once knew a shaman
who talked about time,

the slippery way
it moved, similar to how
profound truths slip

past masses. That man
broke down
in quantum

how particles
can be sped up, paused,
slowed at will:

Einstein knew
how time turned
relatively,

slow as molasses
in the center
of tornadoes.

Even he never knew
how to halt
maelstroms of utterances

better retracted.
Oh, for those lost
spoken chances.

# For

I.

Forbearance is a basket of coal on a crow's head.

For when a young woman tells a saint *I love you,* he replies *I must
love all people*, an opportunity for liberation translates as pain. Long after
her babies are born, she remembers.

Clouds graze as cows rolling across hills roll. As if they go on to topple
over bluffs that take on the sun's brightness
as it sets.

Forsake the idea of the sun setting. This fiery star never rises or
dips: an illusion minds cast into
preset frames.

II.

Form: your real one is as plural formlessness.

Forego all that does not give pleasure. Indulge in self-discipline
or Bacchanalian erotica; your tallow drips,
kindling diminishes quick.

Forthright, be as the grove that gives first press from fallen
olives. Get rid of those pits so that virgin oil runs your throat
into warbles.

Forgive yourself.

III.

Foremost, be *Aletheia.* Be that flash when earth juts through
the busy world's mantle.

Foreswear Zirconia for pebbles that ignite your spirit—you can hold them always
in the curl of your palm.

Forfeit all pretense you are not a sacred forest. Give up
any notion you are not loved.

Force is a weapon to be reckoned with. Forgive me.

IV.

Forward—cast your eyes there. Or keep them here. Toast each morning
with your mug—today is your birthday.

Fortune is culled by what we call from our energy,
despite nature as predatory. I've learned this watching birds rotate,
sharks orbit, people enclosing on subways,
eyes hungry.

Foresee your death. Feel it touch the back of your neck. Grab, smash
it against your fear.

For I was a woman who loved all people.

*Free ~~from~~ Kuwait*


My youth wafts up in incensed breaths:
*Nag Champa*, stale cigarettes, musk of rage, exhaled
from the folds of a black sweatshirt
exhumed from an old army duffle bag.
                    The 1990s tumble back
into my hands. I untuck sleeves, faint scent of grief rolling from cuffs
as I reread the block text then hold the shirt to my chest, allowing its darkness
to hug me once more.
                    The past oscillates. Times I wore this top like a banner,
its colored message matching the Kuwaiti flag. Exiled, but never an exile,
the shirt is a portal, channeling the selves I grew into
then shed, now bookended between my hands.


I unravel their semblance like spools of thread,
my fingers gently tracing the third word, stenciled with white-out


in the middle,
no longer a fit.

# I've Come Back for My Clothes

*At Notre Dame* ∞

Those tattered rags in a glass case
belonging to a nameless saint
are mine,

those cherubs in ceiling corners
looking down on us
are real.

If I stood behind the pulpit
and prayed out loud
while looking up into the palm

of a stained glass dome,
who's to say I haven't stood here before,
even before these marble floors

were grouted and laid?
We learn about dying from the dead
in the form of a chain, of one long

chain, outside the circle of linear minds.
We all once knew the secret handshake,
the firm grip of hands

outside of time.
So tell me, dear Cynthia: who's to say
these clothes aren't mine?

# A Different Kind of Hajj

i.

I have traveled so long,
walked the map of 99 names
chiseled along my palms,

traced backs of sand dunes
and followed its calligraphy

I have come all this way
from the past and future I

sprang from the fertile crescent
to the house of Abraham,
have traveled so long
to find you.

You have led me,
as you led Abraham
through the desert
to build my own house.

ii.

Beyond
the Illuminated City,
a pebbled moon
reveals itself
in wedges,

as do you
come forth and are
interpreted

as different anthems
to those who are listening,
each like granite

with one hand
over the heart.

iii.

Once, I went
to the Louvre's third wing,
saw statues of basalt
and marble, others
in gold leaf,

some with hands
over the heart:

echoes along the annals
of the many.

iv.

I am
in Afghanistan
standing before two Buddha
carved into a sandstone cliff,
faces of the great spirit
imprinted in rock and

mote.

v.

I have come, again,
come from the Seine
and Mississippi, Tigris
and Euphrates
I have journeyed
down the Nile
to Mecca and el-Ka'aba,
the world's navel,
to witness 360
manifestations
within it.

I have come
from Diana and Isis

I am

a mirror to the galaxy.

vi.

I Name Them:

*Hubal,* as father,
*Manat, Uzza, Al-Lat,*
son and daughters.

Moon God *Amm*:

I am

the crescent
on the minaret.

vii.

What is the Holy
Why circumambulation
When were the Days of Ignorance

Who are the moistened stones?

viii.

I have come all this way
with my own elixir,
traveled so long
as my own meteor,

past the *Kuf'far*
and the *Believers*

to kiss your black stone.

ix.

*Allah,*

Giver

of rain, we pray
for the blessing

of rain.

# Travel Guide
*Mahboula, Kuwait, 2017*

I see God twirling in the streets
between plastic wrappers and wind-scattered tissue paper
in dumpsters piled high with cat-clawed garbage bags

spilling treasures like piñatas. I see God running
with packs of wild dogs, coming inland at dawn from the seashore,
glint of divinity in their flint eyes taking in new high rise

construction sites I can hear Him in the caesuras
among the tide-slapping waves and glugs of cement mixers, hear Him
under the Mercurial blaze of the climbing sun

I find God blowing down rows of parked buses
whose metal hulks cart migrant workers to and from daily grind shifts
I find Him shining from two pairs of Benec seed eyes, Lovebirds

caged above a window, in their lovesick muster to continue
in spite their lack of sky view. I see Her in the foamy lips of sea
spitting up plastic bottles on beaches,

find Her in the froth of acidic peninsula brine,
pitted in its dead coral, or etched in the fractal-patterned backs
of emptied sea shells designating infinity,

You can see God across the sun-drenched stony faces
of Nepalese cleaners inadvertently washed up by economic necessity
and cast into new uniformed trajectories of subservience

to alpha male citizens and their female, power corona'd proxies
but I do see, I do I must I do, even when I can't bear to look hear or listen
I find God even in pixelated air, held hostage

when reverberating with calls to prayer, haunting and beautiful
until its repetitive coercion into ears turns sublime into ugly. Despite myself
I see Them It Him Her Whatever casted Pronoun or Name

deified in all faces, seas of sand grains, in multitudes of definitions we squabble
over.

# Singular Notes

This lamenting is not
discordant pianos. It isn't heavy

metal elevator music,
blocking out daybreak twitter.

My keens like glass shatter
beneath trees, dissolve

between sonic pulse
and static AM/FM frequencies.

Fracture in quiet.
Across the World Wide Web.

Branches scold in wind.
My shattered chords

seek assemblage
against dystopian backdrops,

browse *Sheet Music for Dummies*
manuals, self-paced how-to's:

*Play the Guitar in 3 Days*
*Dismantle a Planet in 4 Decades*

Do you remember driving
under a blue moonrise

we slapped our thighs, sang
*remember elevators?*

Just tell me where do I click now
what operatic notes to pitch

or drop, over the ground
for us to listen.

I can't make up my mind:
are these voices yours

or mine?
I can't tell, over and over

and over the shriek
of a garbage bag in the back

car seat. Oh the static.
Oh the sounds we heard. Do you

remember: we slapped our thighs,
singing, *remember birds?*

photo by Adrienne Mathiowetz

Eman Hassan is a bicultural poet from Massachusetts and Kuwait. Her debut collection of poetry, *Raghead* received a Folsom Award and was the Editor's Choice in the 2018 New Issues Poetry Prize. An Arizona State University and University of Nebraska alumnus, Eman currently lives in the Pacific Northwest.

# The New Issues Editor's Choice